POPPA

THE ENTREPRENEUR WHO KNEW HOW TO SPICE THINGS UP

RAVE BOOKS

Poppadom had come up the hard way.

He'd been at it for years slaving for his tiny tip while working long hours as a waiter.

He took pride in everything he did, and everybody said he gave great service.

Poppadom was in demand.

He was offered the top job at the finest Indian restaurant in the land.

But he'd always wanted to make it big on his own.

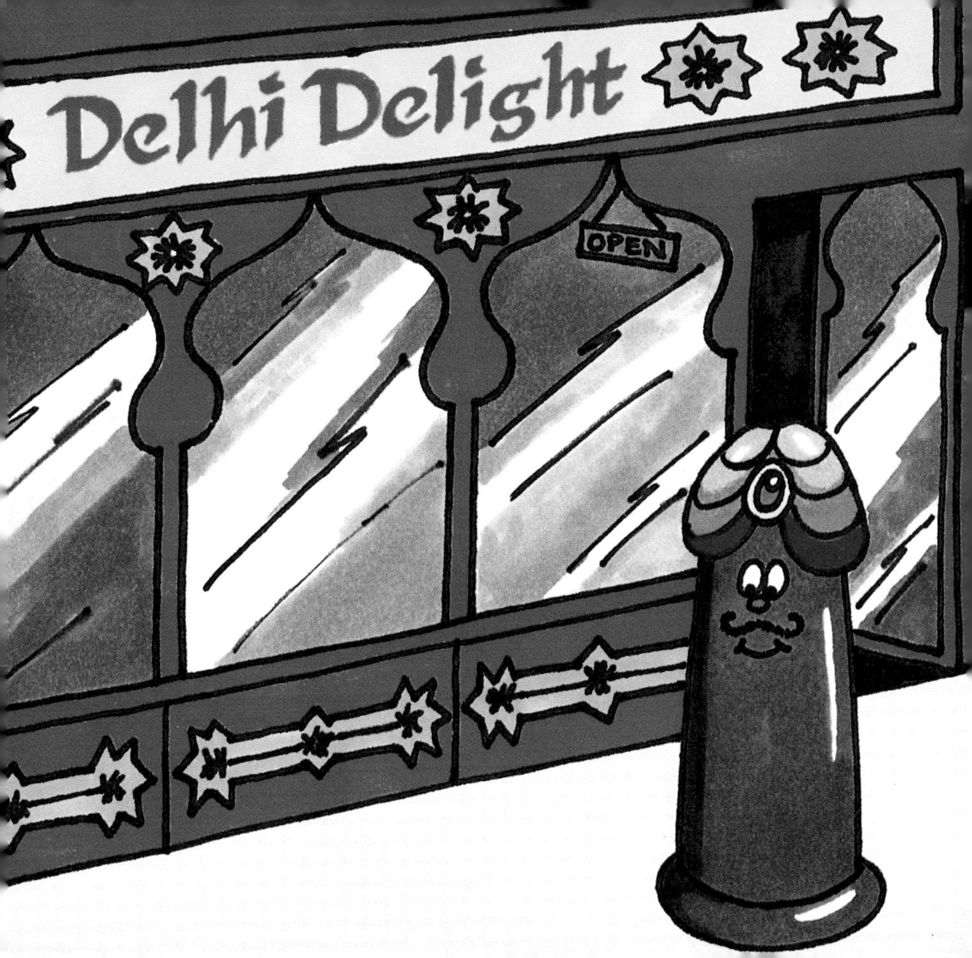
Delhi Delight
OPEN

And now it was time to make things happen,
with a spurt of inspiration.

And a helping hand from his girlfriend,
Donna Kebab.

Tonight was Poppadom's big night.

It was the launch of his sensational new venture 'Planet Poppadom'.

People were coming from all over the place.

They wanted to experience the hottest opening ever.

But there was still a lot to do.

Poppadom was in the goods area getting to grips with his end of things.

"I'll give you a hand with the deliveries," said Donna.

So they got stuck in and humped away together for over an hour.

Finally, they had off-loaded the last of the chutney.

"That's finished me off," Poppadom gasped, straightening up.

"Me too!" sighed Donna.

Yet they kept at it.

By six o'clock Poppadom and Donna's efforts left nothing to be desired.

Everything was all laid out.

The last candle was slotted into place, and Planet Poppadom opened with a bang.

It was amazing.

The stars began to arrive in their long limousines.

Wave after wave of them.

Each bigger than the last.

They just kept on coming…
          and coming…
                 and coming.

Nookie Boldberg and Mell Givesome headed straight for Poppadom's Karma Sutra Cocktail Bar.

"Wow! so many titillatingly tipples," said Nookie, as she read the menu.

"What do you fancy?" she asked.

"The 69 sounds delicious," Mell replied.

"I'll join you!" said Nookie, with a mouthful of nuts.

They were slurping away at their cocktails when
The Kinkies came on stage.

Their act was followed by Spank Me Fred,
Glory Estefanny and a cracking performance from
Whipme Whostun.

Some celebrities got up to dance.

So did Stiff Richards and Marlina Nippleova.

"I like a good groove," said Stiff Richards
to anyone who was listening.

Donna began taking food orders.

Arny Shaftsalotbigger, Brute Willies and Lester Stallion were ravenous.

"Yo, Donna. Let's taste your Moist Madras," shouted Stallion.

"Do you like it hot?" Willies asked.

"The hotter the better," said Shaftsalotbigger, licking his lips.

Poppadom's succulent sauces were going down
a treat with the ladies.

"Just lurve those meatballs," drooled Madomma.

"And I can taste fresh cumin," said Cathlean Turnon.

"Ooooh heaven, my favourite," sighed Moan Collinz.

"It's a matter of personal taste," observed Poppadom as he moved to the next table.

"What will it be gentlemen?" he asked.

"I'll have the Divine Dansak," ordered Lewd Grunt.

"A savoury Slap 'n Tickle Mesala for me," said Donny DeBonko.

"And I'll have anything," said Small Screwman.

"On a bed of Pillow Rice?" enquired Poppadom.

"Just as it comes," they all replied.

"The service is excellent," Raquelle Squelch squealed.

"Thank you," said Poppadom.
"Now what can I offer you?"

"We'll share the Chef's Sheathed Samosa," said Sohorny Beaver.

And they weren't disappointed.

In fact it was so filling, they each bought an 'I love being stuffed at Planet Poppadom' T-shirt on the way out.

Then everyone wanted a souvenir T-shirt.

"I want a large one," said Jody Frothier.

"Then, try mine for size," said Kelvin Cossiter.

"That'll do nicely, but I must get a cap first," she said reaching for the Planet Poppadom baseball cap.

Soon everyone had got what they were after –
and went home satisfied.

Well, almost everyone.

"Have you enjoyed yourselves, gentlemen?"
Poppadom asked the last remaining customers
at a corner table.

The men looked up from their Bulging Bhajis.
"Yes thank you," they said.

"Would you like a cocktail, on the house?"
asked Donna as she approached.

"No thank you. But we'd like to give you something,"
said the men showing their impressive credentials.

Poppadom and Donna couldn't believe their eyes.

The men were the famous Rude Brothers.

"Planet Poppadom is out of this world.
It's the best restaurant we've been to," they said.
"We award you The Purple Pole of Perfection."

Then they picked up their coats,
bought a T-shirt each, and left.

"Well blow me!" said Poppadom.

"Here's to your brilliant idea," said Donna.

And to celebrate she treated Poppadom
to something really hot and spicy...

that wasn't on the menu.